ATHENA

GODDESS OF WAR AND WISDOM

Manuela Dunn Mascetti

GODDESS WISDOM

CHRONICLE BOOKS
SAN FRANCISCO

A Labyrinth Book

First published in the United States in 1996 by Chronicle Books.

Copyright © 1996 by Labyrinth Publishing (UK) Ltd.

Design by DW Design.

All rights reserved. No part of this book may be reproduced without written permission from the Publisher.

The Little Wisdom Library–Athena–Goddess of War and Wisdom was produced by Labyrinth Publishing (UK) Ltd. Printed and bound in Hong Kong.

Library of Congress Cataloging-in-Publication Data: Athena, Goddesses of Wisdom.

Dunn Mascetti, Manuela

Athena—Goddess of War and Wisdom by Manuela Dunn Mascetti.

p. cm.

Includes bibliographical references.

ISBN 0–8118–0914–5

1. Athena (Greek deity) 2. Archetype (Psychology). 3. Mythology, Greek–Psychological aspects. 4. Feminity (Psychological) 5. Women–Psychology. I. Title.

BL820. M6D86 1996

292.2' 114–dc20   95–11654
                     CIP

Distributed in Canada by Raincoast Books,
8680 Cambie Street, Vancouver, B.C. V6P 6M9

10 9 8 7 6 5 4 3 2 1

CHRONICLE BOOKS

275 FIFTH STREET, SAN FRANCISCO, CA 94103
CHRONICLE BOOKS ® IS REGISTERED IN THE U.S. PATENT AND TRADEMARK OFFICE.

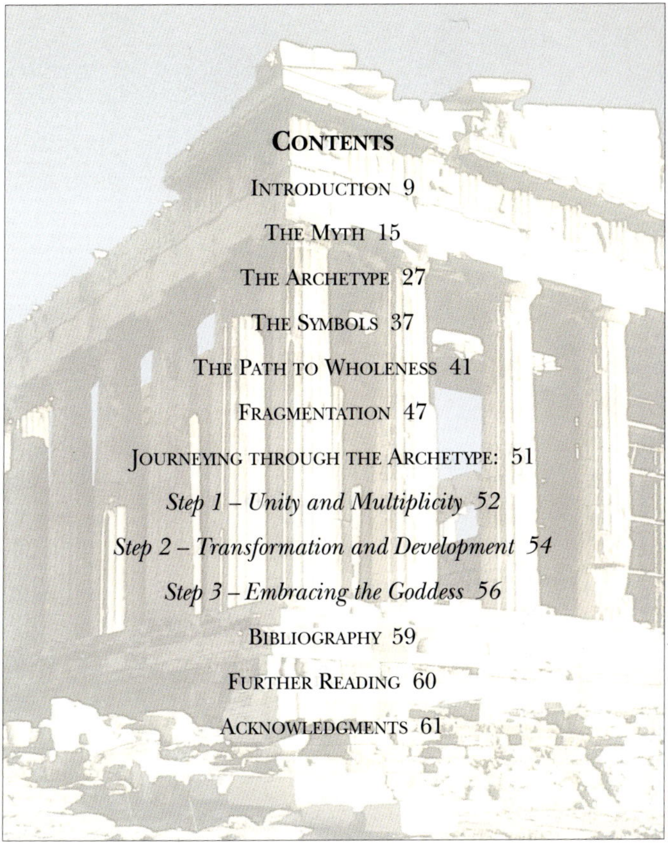

CONTENTS

INTRODUCTION 9

THE MYTH 15

THE ARCHETYPE 27

THE SYMBOLS 37

THE PATH TO WHOLENESS 41

FRAGMENTATION 47

JOURNEYING THROUGH THE ARCHETYPE: 51

Step 1 – Unity and Multiplicity 52

Step 2 – Transformation and Development 54

Step 3 – Embracing the Goddess 56

BIBLIOGRAPHY 59

FURTHER READING 60

ACKNOWLEDGMENTS 61

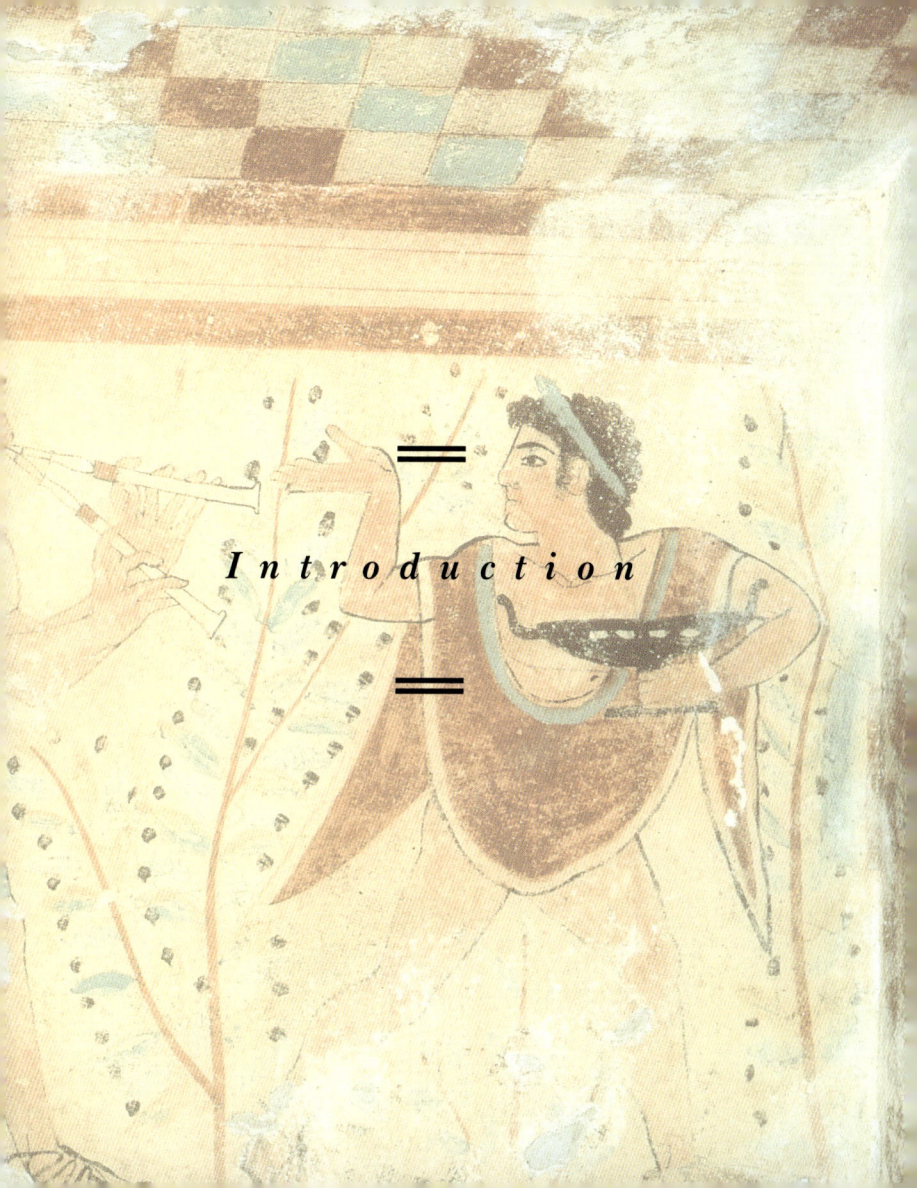

Introduction

ATHENA—GODDESS OF WAR AND WISDOM

In the analysis and interpretation of mythology, we recognize mythological concepts as symbols which recur in our everyday lives. The Olympian goddesses had very human attributes; their behavior, emotional reactions, and mythological conduct provide us with patterns that parallel human behavior and actions. Their stories resonate at a deep level also because they represent archetypes, models of being and behaving we recognize in the collective unconscious. These patterns were first studied by Carl G. Jung, and when manifested in the form of mythical goddesses, they provide modern woman with a key to recognize similar qualities within her self. By exploring ancient myths and their symbols we can explore the depths of our psyche.

Hestia, Artemis, and Athena were the three virgin goddesses who appeared in Greek mythology. The modern concept of virginity is that of celibacy and abstinence from sexual contact, but these three goddesses were set apart from their female counterparts for a completely different reason: in the case of the virgin goddesses, the term "virginity" refers to their emotional life, attitude, and outlook; it does not refer to a physical state or lack of experience.

The life of a woman in ancient Greece was divided artificially into two very distinct periods: virginity and marriage. Once married, a

INTRODUCTION

woman became the responsibility of her husband, but whilst she was single, she belonged to herself alone. It is this virginal quality of "one-in-herself," as Esther Harding first outlined in her book *Woman's Mysteries*, that is the more accurate description of the virgin goddesses.

Few female divinities represent this quality; most are merely the counterparts of male gods from whom they derive both their power and prestige, and they personify that aspect of feminine nature which is dependent upon and balanced by male energy. Artemis, Hestia, and Athena have no husbands or lovers to control or determine their qualities, and are thus their own mistresses.

Their functions, symbols, and rites belong to themselves alone; they represent the essence of the pure feminine.

Frontispiece: Minerva and the Centaur, by Botticelli, *c.*1480.
Previous pages: Servants and musicians in a fifth–century B.C. Etruscan wall painting, Tarquinia Italy.
Above: Athena wearing her war helmet, a fifth-century B.C. statue now in the Louvre Museum, Paris.

ATHENA—GODDESS OF WAR AND WISDOM

The goddess Athena is motivated by her own priorities and sets her own standards. The only goddess to wear armor, she is portrayed always with her helmet pushed back to reveal her face. She carries a shield on her arm and often has an owl sitting on her shoulder, which symbolizes her wisdom. The key word for Athena is *illumination:* instinct is filtered through her intellect, resulting in her cool, clear view. Unlike Artemis and Hestia, Athena seeks the company of men and helps them in strategies of war. She enjoys being in the midst of male action and power, but in times of peace, she turns to the more stereotypically feminine aspect of her nature and presides over the creative arts and crafts. Athena's critical abilities, precise-

Above: A bronze statue of Athena, originally adorning the Acropolis in Athens, Greece.
Opposite: Spinning and weaving were associated with Athena, under her goddess patronage of the arts and crafts.

INTRODUCTION

ness, and wisdom have been glorified in myth. She is independent and trustworthy, and she is the protector of cities, the patron of military forces, and goddess of weavers, dressmakers, goldsmiths, and potters. As an archetype in women's psychology, Athena motivates persistence, determination, and achievement of goals. The Athena woman seems to have been born to enjoy responsibility, and she possesses a magnetic personal intensity. She exudes power and understands how to use it, both to promote and prevent change. She is, above all, a strategist, able to determine with extreme clarity the shortest path to the goal, and she often makes a great impact upon the world.

The Myth

ATHENA—GODDESS OF WAR AND WISDOM

Athena, known in Roman mythology as Minerva, was worshipped in ancient Greece as goddess of war and wisdom, as well as goddess of arts and crafts. She was the patron goddess of Athens and, as a virgin goddess, was strong and self-sufficient, equal to all male gods of Mount Olympus. Her physical virginity was emblematic of the invincibility of the city.

Greek mythologians were ambivalent about the sex of their gods: were the main protagonists of their pantheon to be he- or she-gods? Athena represents a compromise of this debate for, while being female, she incarnates qualities that are masculine. Dressed in armor, a tireless and highly skilled

THE MYTH

strategist in times of war, Athena dwelled in the world of the male gods, only occasionally venturing into the feminine Olympian world to deliver gifts and teach the women crafts to help them better their condition.

Athena's constant companion, both in mythology and in the art that depicted her throughout the centuries, is the owl, a hunting bird and symbol of wisdom. Athena's temple in the Parthenon of Athens was the seat of wisdom not only for her city, but also for the entirety of the Hellenic world. The power of this goddess radiated into the rituals of Greek households and extended into battlegrounds and into the minds of war chieftains.

Previous pages: A colossal statue of Minerva presiding over a temple in Rome.
Opposite: Ingrid Bergman as Joan of Arc, a later incarnation of Athena's principles. *Above:* The owl, Athena's sacred bird—this stone sculpture used to guard the gates of the goddess's temple on the Acropolis.

ATHENA—GODDESS OF WAR AND WISDOM

The Birth of Athena

The lineage of Athena is unclear. Some storytellers say that Athena had a father named Pallas, a goat-like giant with great wings. He attempted to outrage her and she retaliated by killing him, stripping him of his skin and robbing him of his wings—which she immediately affixed to her own shoulders. Others say that Athena's father was the King of Iton; others still say that Poseidon (god of the sea) was her father, whom she disowned, asking to be adopted by Zeus instead. Typically, Athena is attended by priests, not priestesses, and it was her own priests who told the following story about her birth.

Zeus lusted after Metis, who, in an attempt to escape him, transformed herself into many different shapes until at last she was caught and made pregnant by him. An oracle of Mother Earth then predicted that Metis would give birth to a girl; and that if she became pregnant again she would give birth to a boy who would depose Zeus in the same way as he had deposed his father, Cronus, and as Cronus had deposed Uranus. Zeus, alarmed by the ominous message of the oracle, sweet-talked Metis to rest on a couch and, having made her very small, swallowed her, and later claimed that she gave him counsel from his belly.

Months passed and one day Zeus was seized by a raging headache while he

THE MYTH

Above: Mount Olympus, the home of Athena.

ATHENA — GODDESS OF WAR AND WISDOM

was walking on the shores of Lake Triton. The pain was such that it seemed to him his skull would burst and he howled with rage until the whole firmament echoed with his cries. Hermes and Hephaestus came to Zeus's help. The latter cracked Zeus's skull with a mighty blow of his ax; and with a great cry, Athena sprang, fully armed, out of the breach.

This mythological account implies that Zeus gave birth to Athena by a very mental, quasi-cesarean birth. It is not surprising that Athena possessed the gifts of purposeful thinking and practicality: her mother, Metis, was a Titan, and guardian of the planetary power of Mercury which was associated with wisdom. Athena was always able to plan strategies and guide them to their execution, and so achieve tangible, positive results. This goddess valued rational thinking highly, and believed in the superiority of will and intellect over instinct.

THE MYTH

Athena's Deeds

Athena invented the flute, the trumpet, the earthenware pot, the plough, the rake, the ox-yoke, the bridle, the chariot, and the ship. She first taught the science of numbers, and all women's arts, such as cooking, weaving, and spinning. Although a goddess of war, she gets no pleasure from battle, as Ares and Eris do, but rather from settling disputes, and upholding the law by pacific means. She bears no arms in time of peace and, if ever she needs any, will usually borrow her weapons from Zeus. Her mercy is great: when the judges' votes are equal in a criminal trial at the Areiopagus, she always gives a casting vote to liberate the accused. Yet, once engaged in battle, she never loses the day, even against Ares himself, being better grounded in tactics and strategy than he; and wise captains have always approached her for advice.

Opposite: Mourning Athena.
Above: A woman sewing—Athena, although an excellent war strategist, was also the patron of women's arts and crafts.

ATHENA — GODDESS OF WAR AND WISDOM

Athena was the goddess consulted in times of war and uncertainty; her mind was unwavering and she did not hesitate to take action, however ruthless it seemed.

One night, Medusa, one of the Gorgons, daughters of the sea, was making love to Poseidon in one of Athena's temples. When Athena found them out, she was enraged that they would dare to desecrate her sacred space. To prevent any risk of it happening again, she changed Medusa into a winged monster with glaring eyes, a protruding tongue, and brazen claws. Her hair she made into a myriad of writhing snakes, whose gaze turned men to stone. It fell to the hero Perseus to kill the Medusa, but before facing her he asked his friends for help. Hermes gave him a curved sword and winged sandals, Athena gave him a mirror-shield, and Hades gave him a helmet which made its wearer invisible. Thus equipped, Perseus slew Medusa, avoiding being turned into stone by watching her reflection in the mirror-shield. From the pregnant Medusa's neck, Pegasus and Chrysaor were released, and Athena fastened Medusa's head to her shield.

Athena's myths have often been interpreted to show the goddess siding with patriarchy. When Orestes killed Clytemnestra, his mother, in order to avenge the murder of his father, Agamemnon, Apollo took it upon himself to defend Orestes. To prove his inno-

THE MYTH

Above: The head of Medusa in a floor mosaic in a Roman villa in Morocco.

ATHENA—GODDESS OF WAR AND WISDOM

cence, Apollo declared that motherhood was unimportant, asserting that a woman was no more than a vessel for the man to deposit his seed. He cited Athena, who had been born from her father's brow with little help from her mother. It was a passionate, well-argued debate, and when the jury's vote was found to be equal, Athena was called upon to give the casting vote, as was traditional in such cases. Although rational and calculating, one of her greatest attributes is that of according mercy to the accused or condemned, and as she had done at so many other trials where her opinion was sought, she voted in favor of the accused. Amidst scenes of great triumph, Orestes was set free, and Athena thus decided the result of the first trial in history where patriarchy triumphed.

THE MYTH

Athena came to the aid of heroes because they were worthy of her esteem, not because of any amorous attraction—her heart remained insensitive to the pangs of love, despite the fact that many fell in love with her. Among them was Hephaestus, Aphrodite's husband. One day, when the goddess consulted him about a new suit of armor which she needed, he attempted to rape her. Athena fled, pursued by the limping god. Eventually he caught her, but she defended herself so effectively that Hephaestus could not possess her. Instead, he scattered his seed on the earth, which shortly after gave birth to a son. Athena found the child and brought him up secretly; she hid the infant in a basket which she entrusted to the daughters of Cecrops, commanding them not to open it. Two of the three sisters, however, could not resist the curiosity of discovering what was in the basket, and when they opened it they fled in terror, because coiled around the child was a poisonous snake. The child, called Erichthonius, grew to become a king of Athens, where he established the cult of Athena.

Opposite: A bronze statue of Athena, the warrior goddess, patroness of the arts.

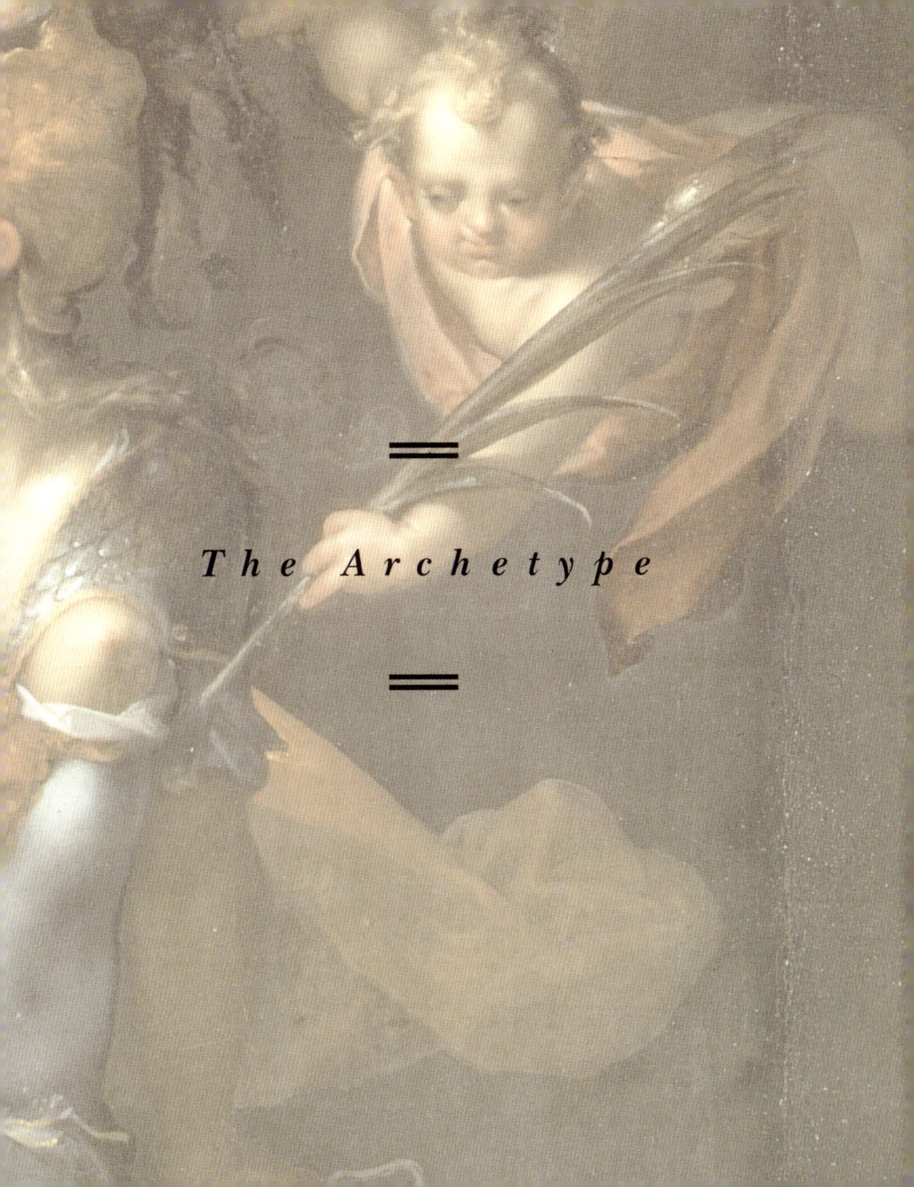

The Archetype

ATHENA—GODDESS OF WAR AND WISDOM

Athena is a father's daughter, born from her father's brow "fully armed" and with a mighty shout that must have sounded like a war cry. As goddess of war and wisdom, Athena helped mortals and male gods alike with her excellent strategies and careful planning. As an archetype, Athena is present in those women who use rational thinking, logic, and clear intuition as their discerning tools for life. Athena's archetype teaches us that the ability to be rational and clearheaded, rather than emotional, and to be able to respond positively and constructively to conflicts and challenges, are characteristics shared, to some degree, by most women. In Athena, masculine and feminine characteristics are perfectly

Previous pages: Minerva Triumphs over Ignorance, a painting by Bartholomaus Spranger (1546–1611).
Above: Athena as she stood on the Parthenon—this statue was sculpted by Phidias.

THE ARCHETYPE

balanced, and whenever the goddess is portrayed with another figure, that figure is always a male god. This rational/emotional balance is displayed perfectly in right and left brain psychology: the left-brain is rational, verbal, and linear, while the right-brain is non-rational, nonverbal, and nonlinear. Wisdom, Athena shows us, is achieved by equalizing these two realms within our heart and mind—within our psyche.

It is important for the woman in whom Athena is an active archetype to recognize her mental powers as a positive characteristic, rather than fearing that these may have been adopted from men in order to compete with them. Athena consciousness promotes the one-in-herself quality of the virgin, enabling us to accept the company of men as colleagues or companions without letting erotic feelings or emotional intimacy cloud our relationships. By developing our understanding of Athena, we reveal a positive image of a strong, powerfully attractive femininity which is unaffected or even enhanced by, rather than wounded or lessened by, male presence.

In the myth we learn that the goddess also possessed practical acumen, inventing a number of devices with which to tame Nature, such as the bridle for use in both war and agriculture, and the ship to explore unknown lands and increase trade of commodities.

ATHENA — GODDESS OF WAR AND WISDOM

Athena as an archetype displays maturity, wisdom, and responsibility. She may lack romanticism and high idealism, but instead she is pragmatic and realistic, bringing to us practical strategies and devices.

The Qualities of Athena

- **Virginal and independent:** is complete within herself, relates to others with equality

- **Incisive and focused:** sees situations and people for what they are, rather than what they should be

- **Organized, responsible, critical, and efficient:** achieves her goals through clarity and careful planning; acts swiftly, but is not impulsive

- **Selective, honest, hard-working:** demanding yet generous in spirit

- **A natural leader,** especially in times of turmoil and emotional confusion

- **Excellent and trustworthy friend** to both men and women, her wise counsel is often sought to solve personal conflicts

- **Compassionate:** has a deep need to work with others

THE ARCHETYPE

The Strategist

Athena the war strategist is more excited by planning and results than by battle. She is manifest in women in all those professions which demand an acutely refined and piercing intelligence. The innate wisdom of the archetype, coupled with her swift understanding, makes the woman who embraces the Athena archetype turn everything she handles to gold. But even though this is a powerfully striking archetype, Athena sometimes seems almost to lack personal ambition: she focuses on achieving balance and harmony rather than personal gain. But with this focus, whatever she is organizing will probably end up being all the more successful.

Opposite: Athena with her shield on which the head of Medusa was carved. *Above:* Joan of Arc, a historical incarnation of Athena consciousness.

ATHENA—GODDESS OF WAR AND WISDOM

Athena's acumen helps us bring to fruition the projects we start and helps us achieve what we want in life within the boundaries of what we know we are all capable of.

This archetype, whether functioning alone or with others, encourages a woman to be compelled by priorities—she follows her own visions rather than the dreams of others. As a mature virgin goddess (Athena was born an adult and enjoyed no childhood), she derives a deep, rewarding pleasure from achievement. One of the strengths this archetype provides for modern women is the ability to feel completely comfortable in the world of commerce and industry. Protected by Athena's armor—whether intellectual, professional, or emotional—they are incredible strategists who are able to remain focused on their goals and cannot be distracted until the results are achieved.

Opposite: Weaving is a metaphor for the passing of time and the interlocking of events.

THE ARCHETYPE

The Goddess of Arts and Crafts

Athena created items that were useful and beautiful to behold. She was praised for her skills as a weaver, and weaving is a metaphor for the passing of time, the interlocking of events. The practicality and certainty of this archetype brings us balance and insight. In times of quiet, Athena turns her attention inwards and develops a reservoir of resilience from which she draws in times of turmoil. Athena energy enables a woman to regenerate by dedicating herself to useful and simple tasks—pottery, weaving, tapestry, and playing music. Athena works best for us when we are exhausted by the demands of daily life—when we give ourselves solitude and silence, and time to unravel our thoughts.

ATHENA — GODDESS OF WAR AND WISDOM

Athena's Inner Balance

As an archetype, Athena brings the gift of inner balance, a sign of great strength and maturity. One of the gifts of this archetype is knowing the wisdom of moderation and how to walk the middle-path: highly demanding commitments are counterbalanced by simple tasks; work which dictates high energy and hours of strategic planning is balanced by solitude and silence. Strong and intense emotions, illogical passions, and unconscious fears are the antithesis of rational Athena.

Athena was also worshipped as the goddess of health. The Athena woman maintains a balance between her mind, body, and spirit, knowing this to be essential in order for her to act effectively. She avoids excess in everything: food, drink, emotions, and work.

The sign of Athena is a triangle placed upon a reversed cross, a symbol of her inner direction and self-knowledge. She balances her outer self—that confident and achieving exterior—with her private self, which she keeps veiled from others and which is a constant, essential source of psychic regeneration.

Opposite: The spider, a symbol of the goddess.

THE ARCHETYPE

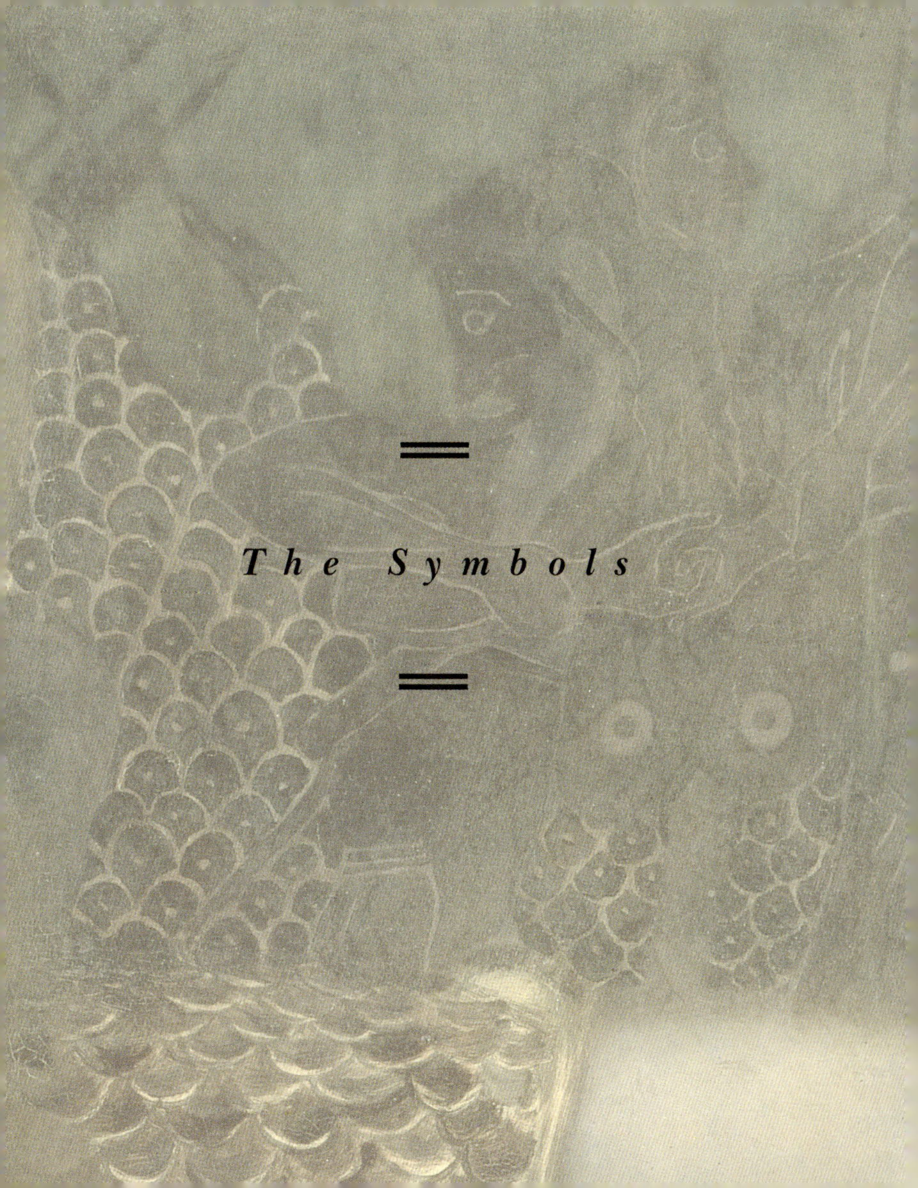

The Symbols

ATHENA — GODDESS OF WAR AND WISDOM

The Symbols of the Goddess

The Owl

As a night bird, the owl was believed to be the bird of the dead. Its love of darkness and its quizzical, pensive look made the owl into a symbol of wisdom, penetrating the darkness of ignorance.

Medusa

Medusa was the only mortal sister of the Gorgons. She is identified as Athena's alter ego; that part of her which can freeze others into terrified stupor.

Previous pages: Pallas Athene by Gustav Klimt. *Above:* The owl and the Medusa, two powerful symbols of Athena.

THE SYMBOLS

The Gorgoneion

The grotesque, horrific head of a Gorgon. The Gorgoneion was affixed to temple doors and to Athena's shield and was a symbol of the terrifying aspects of divinity.

Weaving

A metaphor for the weaving of time, the passing of events, and the workings of the powers of Fate.

Above, left: The Gorgon head in a clay tablet from the temple of Apollo in Villa Giulia, Rome, seventh century B.C. *Above, right:* A woven shawl.

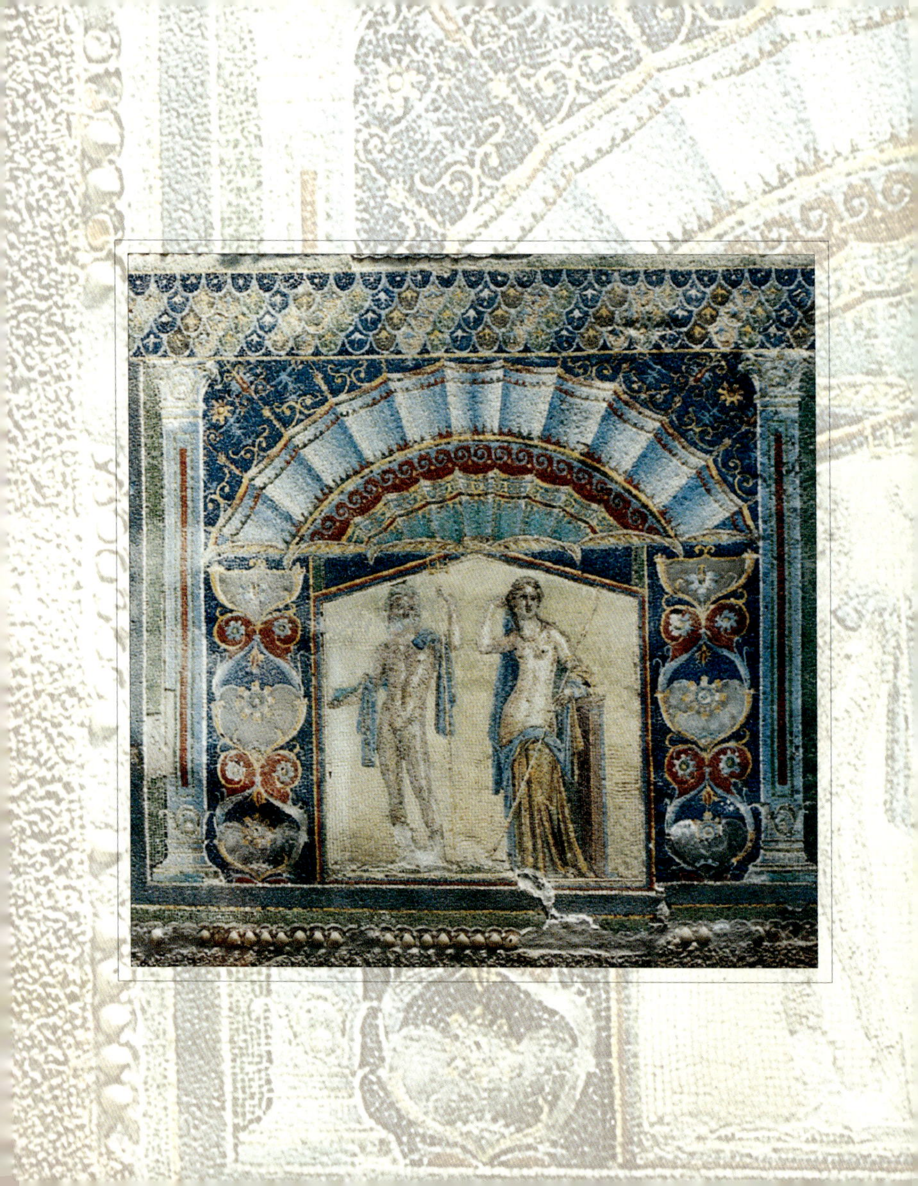

The Path to Wholeness

ATHENA—GODDESS OF WAR AND WISDOM

Athena was born of her father's brow and was motherless from even before her birth. This aspect of her life stands as a metaphor for a difficulty that the woman in whom this archetype is dominant experiences from an early age: she usually lacks close friendships with other women and finds it almost impossible to form close bonds with her female friends. This lack of kinship with other women may have started in her childhood, when her only role model was her father.

The path to wholeness for Athena entails recovering awareness of her mother. Although Athena's mother was literally swallowed by patriarchy, she still exists, albeit somewhat remotely, as a guide and mentor. Similarly, it is possible for all of us—even those among us who are literally motherless—to discover and understand the warmth of maternal love. It is important for all women who recognize the presence of Athena within to remember this.

The presence of the mother figure can be found along many of the different paths of growth: by embracing motherhood, by falling in love, by daring to be vulnerable in the presence of another. Mother can also be found by taking the journey back to the world of childhood, to the point where she was lost in our psyche, understanding, this time with adult intelligence, the trauma that caused us to forget she was there, and which has left us feeling

THE PATH TO WHOLENESS

Previous pages: Athena with Hercules in a mosaic on a Roman temple. *Above:* A Greek sculpture of Athena from her temple on the Acropolis in Athens, Greece.

ATHENA—GODDESS OF WAR AND WISDOM

unmothered ever since. The true feeling of mothering does not come solely from our physical mothers but from the mother in our own self—we need to give her room in our psyche where she can live, to nourish and encourage her, and to honor her presence.

Cultivating Athena means developing and displaying some of her qualities. In work, for instance, Athena uses rational logic, rather than emotional intuition. She examines each task carefully and assesses the amount of time and preparation needed for its completion. She meets deadlines and objectives well prepared, and behaves professionally at all times, putting forth her views skillfully, impersonally, and clearly.

In private, Athena can be cultivated by purposefully planning time for one's self. The Athena woman is attentive to her need for regeneration and makes sure to carve out pockets of space for

THE PATH TO WHOLENESS

herself, to create an environment of peace and silence.

Above: Cultivating the Athena archetype means developing and displaying some of her characteristics, which include traditionally feminine activities.

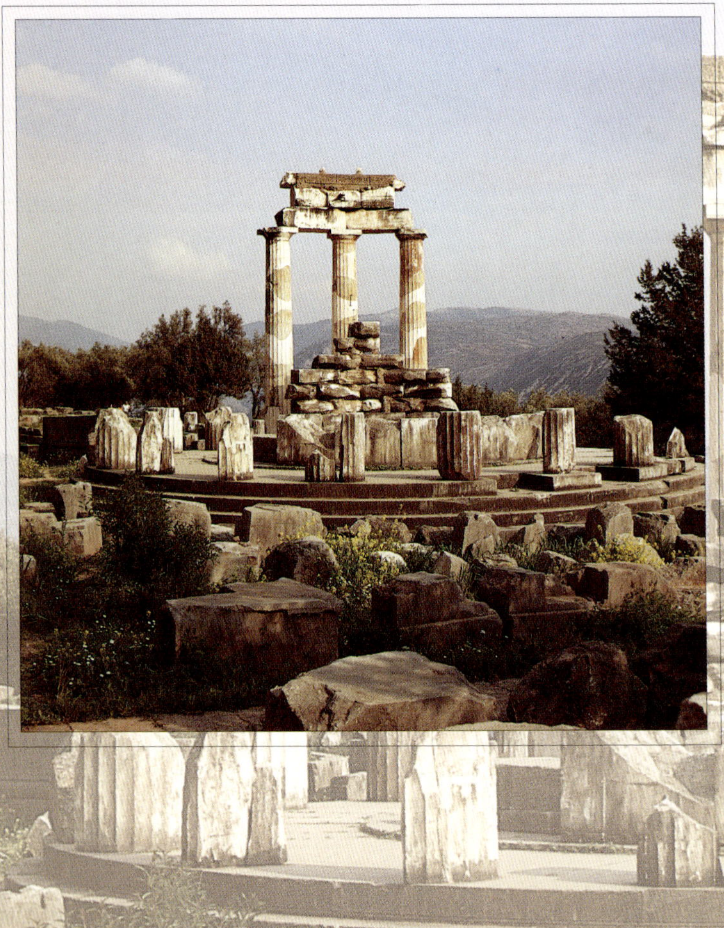

Fragmentation

ATHENA—GODDESS OF WAR AND WISDOM

Fragmentation for the woman who resonates with this archetype occurs when a chasm opens between the rational/emotional, linear/non-linear elements in her psyche. The absence of her mother causes the woman who identifies with Athena a deeply felt anguish. She feels abandoned and betrayed, and is left mistrustful of femininity, fearing the intimacy she has never known.

The woman in whom the Athena archetype is dominant may seek her refuge in logic and rational thought, and can be in danger of losing her spiritual and psychological balance through living such a one-sided existence. She misses many of the experiences which give depth and color to existence: the transporting notes of a beautiful piece of music may leave her unmoved, she may be unable to experience a deep merging during sexual union, she may dismiss feelings by filtering them through her logical mind. She protects herself against excess and loss of purity by adopting the stance of an armored maiden, without realizing that these things against which she protects herself are the very things which could redeem her.

Previous pages: The Tholos of Athena at Delphi, in Greece. *Opposite:* A marble statue of the goddess from the Temple of Aegina, in Greece, 490 B.C.

FRAGMENTATION

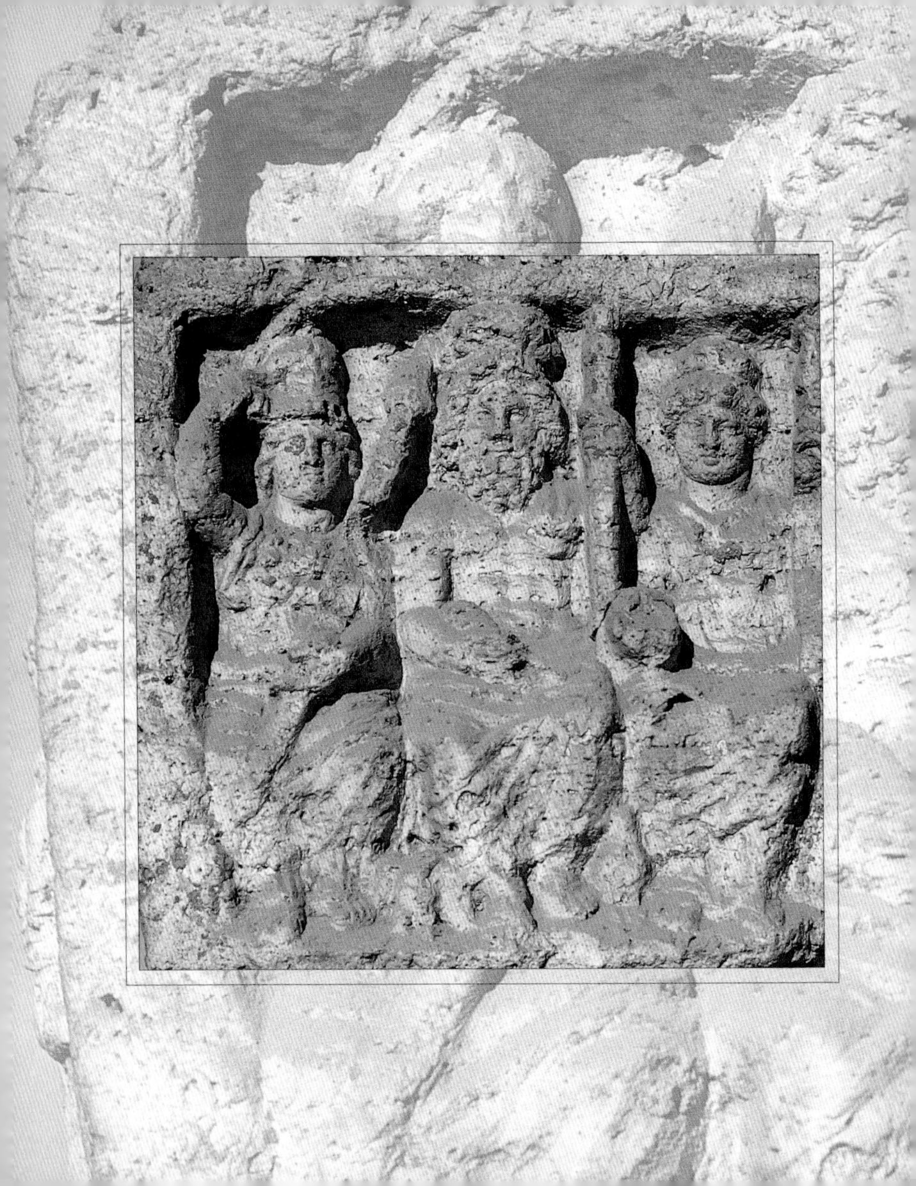

Journeying through the Archetype

Step 1

Unity and Multiplicity

Unity comes to Athena when the goal-oriented, rational principle is balanced by the process-oriented, intuitive forces residing in her psyche. In order to grow out of her armored maidenhood, the woman in whom this archetype is dominant needs to use her ability of focused, rational thought to analyze her need to develop other aspects of herself. Learning to listen to the sensuous, pulsing rhythm of her body is one important tool of self-discovery that will open doors of perception otherwise ignored.

Another way for her to become more self-aware is through paying more attention to the emotions of others. When a friend expresses pain or love, the woman identifying with Athena needs to make an effort to understand and appreciate their feelings. She could perhaps invite them to share some quiet moments with her—these can develop into those precious pockets of life in which we bond deeply with one another. A quiet walk in the woods or a swim in a tranquil pond in the company of one or two close friends can help Athena-consciousness move towards embracing others with flow and grace.

The complete Athena woman, the figure portrayed in the myth, lives in multiplicity. She helps men

JOURNEYING THROUGH THE ARCHETYPE

Previous pages: Minerva, Jupiter, and Juno, the three Roman gods of the Capitol. *Left:* A stone relief showing Athena and Hera honoring the Samians—the goddesses were patrons of their cities.

plan their strategy for war and brings the gift of the arts to women. Modern women who experience the Athena archetype as a strong presence in their lives need to embrace the feminine world as closely as they embrace the masculine; with their acumen and clear-thinking, their potential for greatness—whether in commerce or friendship—can be profound.

ATHENA—GODDESS OF WAR AND WISDOM

Step 2

Transformation and Development

There is one particular episode in the myth which indicates a path for transformation and psychological development: Athena's encounter with Medusa, who begins the tale a lovely girl, but who is soon transformed into a monster by the goddess.

Above: The exploration of Athena's archetype entails growing out of armored maidenhood.
Opposite: Athena helps Perseus kill the Gorgon from whose head Pegasus is born.

Medusa is Athena's symbolic alter-ego. When touched by Athena, Medusa herself transforms and turns men into stone. This is the effect that many women in whom this archetype is dominant may have upon others, intimidating them to such an extent that all conversation, spontaneity, and ease cease with her presence. In her insistence to regard everything rationally, logically, and unemotionally, the woman motivated by Athena energy risks devi-

JOURNEYING THROUGH THE ARCHETYPE

talizing experience, creating for herself a world devoid of passion. She protects this two-dimensional universe by assuming the role of judge, delivering harsh sentences upon others who appear to be less than perfect—to her, at least.

The Medusa represents the realm of the unconscious, the instincts from which Athena is divorced. Irrationality, intuition, darkness, and fluidity are some of the Gorgonian traits which Athena denies. When the contents of the unconscious mind are so repressed, they resurface in dreams and nightmares as dangerous figures which demand our attention and remind us of their existence.

The gift that Athena gave Perseus was a mirrored shield. It enabled the hero to aim his sword at Medusa without having to look at her directly, and so to kill her without being turned to stone. The Medusa is the other face of Athena; it is only by recognizing and incorporating her within her psyche that Athena can become whole again.

ATHENA—GODDESS OF WAR AND WISDOM

When she is acknowledged, Medusa can become a powerful ally of the goddess; she endows Athena with an aura of substance and depth, which is far more impressive than her usual clean-cut rationalization. The Medusa, portrayed on the goddess's breastplate, can also serve as a little extra protection in times of danger. But once battle is done, she must remember to take off the armor and pursue more peaceful pastimes.

Step 3

Embracing the Goddess

We come to the end of our journey through the archetype having learned that we must cherish our mother, encounter and accept Medusa, and balance our masculine and feminine principles with equal measure. Athena's mythological companion was the owl, a symbol of wisdom. We should take care to keep him close by our side to act as a guardian throughout our lives.

Women who strongly identify with Athena need to spin and weave, whether practically or metaphorically. They need to know the blissful space of an empty mind, away from strategies and calculations that sometimes seem the only path to success. And they need to return to the mother, honoring her presence within. These modern-day rituals will enable us all to embrace the goddess and walk sure-footed along her path.

JOURNEYING THROUGH THE ARCHETYPE

Above: Journeying through Athena's archetype entails cherishing and treasuring the mysteries of the feminine realm.

ATHENA — GODDESS OF WAR AND WISDOM

BIBLIOGRAPHY

Graves, R. *The Greek Myths.*
London: Penguin Books, 1992.

Harding, E. M. *Woman's Mysteries.*
New York and San Francisco:
Harper & Row, 1971.

Jung, C. G. *Man and His Symbols.*
London: Aldous Books, 1964.

Neumann, E. *The Great Mother.*
New York: Bollingen Foundation,
Princeton University Press, 1963.

Walker, B. *The Woman's
Encyclopedia of Myths and Secrets.*
San Francisco:
HarperSanFrancisco, 1991.

FURTHER READING

Bolen, J. Shinoda. *Goddesses in Everywoman.* New York and San Francisco: Harper & Row Publishers, 1984.

Bolen, J. Shinoda. *Crossing to Avalon.* San Francisco: HarperSanFrancisco, 1994.

Estés, C. Pinkola. *Women Who Run with the Wolves.* New York: Ballantine Books, 1992.

Harding, E. M. *Woman's Mysteries.* New York and San Francisco: Harper & Row, 1971.

Woodman, M. *Addiction to Perfection—The Still Unravished Bride.* Toronto: Inner City Books, 1985.

Woodman, M. *Leaving My Father's House—A Journey to Conscious Femininity.* London: Ebury Press, 1993

Woodman, M. *The Pregnant Virgin—A Process of Psychological Transformation.* Toronto: Inner City Books, 1985.

Woodman, M. *The Ravaged Bridegroom—Masculinity in Women.* Toronto: Inner City Books, 1990.

ACKNOWLEDGMENTS

Picture Acknowledgments:

AKG London, pages: 8; 13—*Spinning and Weaving,* by Swanenburgh; 31—by Charles Lenoir; 36; 54—illustration, Flemish school.

C M Dixon Photo Resources, pages: 11; 12; 14; 17; 20—Acropolis Museum, Athens; 28; 43; 46; 50; 53—Acropolis Museum, Athens; 55—Sicily.

E T Archive, pages: 4; 19—*Sons of Reno,* set design by Max Bruckner; 23; 26; 33—American quilt; 38 (right); 39 (both); 45—*The Mill,* by Edward Burne-Jones; 49.

Sonia Halliday Photographs, page: 30.

Range Pictures Ltd., pages: 7—The Parthenon, Athens; 16; 21—painting by Jacob Laurence; 57—*Dream Shadows,* by Odilon Redon.

Juliette Soester, page: 40.

Tony Stone Images, pages: 35; 38 (left).

Werner Forman Archive Ltd., page: 24—National Museum, Athens.

Text Acknowledgments

The quotes that appear in this book are taken from *The Greek Myths* by Robert Graves (published by Penguin Books, 1992), reprinted here by kind permission of Carcanet Press Limited.